flickering lives

a collection of poetry

Victor Talamini

FREILING
PUBLISHING

Copyright © 2019 by Victor Talamini
First Paperback Edition

Published by Freiling Publishing, a division of Freiling Agency, LLC.

70 Main Street, Suite 23-MEC
Warrenton, VA 20186

www.FreilingPublishing.com

Library of Congress Control Number: 2019905314

ISBN 9781950948000

Printed in the United States of America

Table of Contents

INTRODUCTION

This book of poems chooses to focus the reader on the paradigms and experiences of those growing up in an inner city environment. The good, bad and sometimes confusing views that have caused many to ponder what life might hold for them.

You get to view life as a lonely spectator, anguished by an often violent world thrust upon many, yet dismissed by some who have never experienced the cruel realities known to others. Of course, most readers will acknowledge that beyond the confines of a tortured soul is a world filled with beauty and opportunity just waiting for those who are set free.

The book explores the beauty of nature, the search for the well known illusive love which so often is misunderstood or destroyed by the violent and ruthless world from which there seems to be no escape. The poetry speaks of loneliness and having few recognizable resources to aid in a search for that which offers the chance to find a place of comfort in an otherwise turbulent world.

This book scans life as a child, the teenage years, and the blistering world of factory work. The temptations known to many that have severe consequences fostered by the difficult and sometimes misguided choice.

In this book we navigate through life, and reason when one becomes a thought they should be beauty in someone's life. There is also the anguish found in the nagging reminder that above all, irrespective of relationships, romances, family and friends, one must face life alone, with the choices made or imposed in an ever changing world.

The Price of a Thought

I drift through a field of tall grass,
With a soft warm breeze to my back
enjoying life;
Slender green, featherlike blades grab at
my body as I pass by.

I look up at the sun and laugh
and he smiles down on me
For he is the king of all life
and the thought warms my soul
A single lark has captured the moment
he must tell the world he has lost his
lover
But he has not lost his love,
and the whole meadow understands
his pain;
Even I.

Yet my thoughts flow free like silver ribbons
Blown with the rhythm of a summer
breeze.
With only the sun to compliment their beauty
and the wind to carry their motion:

I followed the sound of a small stream,
When I came upon the stream
I walked in it
My whole body seemed to feel the
excitement of its motion, and its delicate
chill

I pressed my toes to the soft bed below
and my fingers reached toward the sky: If only I could pull it down
over my shoulders:
I would never again want.

But the current took me, and my thoughts
with it
Traveling along her swerving banks,
feeling, touching, tasting a part of
everything along the way;

I traveled on till the meadow saw my back;
I traveled till my face met a new
dawn
And I turned about and the meadow
was gone,
But I still could feel a cool chill
about my feet;
And the sweet taste of a warm summer breeze
upon my tongue
All for the price of a thought.
When I am a thought;
I want to be beauty in somebody's life.

Bananas

Mother moved about the kitchen, bowls clattering, spoons playing on table top and four hungry children clamoring, orchestrated crescendo rising and falling to mothers frantic dance. For one short moment a lapse in orchestrations, watching corn flakes tumble into the first bowl – John's bowl. Then, off in the distance a faint sound; "bananas, bananas", a familiar addition to breakfast sounds. It meant the produce man, his horse and wagon were calling out to all those who had ten cents and a taste for the yellow treat.

Mom said, "John, here, 10 cents, go get a bunch." He refused the honor and pointed to me, five year old Victor. "Make him do it this time". Odd, because John the eldest, 7 years old was always first when it came to anything from a toss of the ball to a peek through a hole in the fence. "Let him go, I do it all the time." He pushed the dime at me and started yelling, "go!", "go"! I started down the long dark, second story stairway. Reaching up, I opened the door a crack and the call grew louder. On the pole near the street was a woodpecker that seemed to be a world away from the noise upstairs as he rapped out his own song in the bright morning sun. I could see the small bugs just awakening from the shadows below my lofty position on the six step porch. There wasn't a lower spot in East Orange or on this street, East Day Street. The horse's pace added a tempo to the woodpecker's beat, to the otherwise quiet street just as the peddler came into view. The voice rang out in a sing, song tempo; "bananas", "bananas" and I didn't know what came next so I put half of my body through the door and mimicked the call in what was a soft sweet voice and the peddler, his horse and wagon, continued on down the street. So I raised my voice a bit louder and opened my small hand to show the much valued dime. Once again I called and the peddler turned and looked sharply at me as if he were annoyed, his spoiled gray hat and thick dark eye brows frightened me. The peddler never stopped his rhythmic call nor interrupted his horse's cadence as they proceeded down the street.

The woodpecker continued to drum as I looked on, knowing my opportunity had passed and there would be no bananas today. I started my unhappy retreat up the stairs to face the music, empty handed. I had failed them and would not be trusted with such an important job in the future. I didn't know how John did it but John always came back with a bunch.

The Flower

Such beauty found in a flower, a delicate life, mixed color, shapes of all
sizes birth and demises
They bring joy to the hungry eye, to the empty landscape
To the lonely so love does not die
When I look about, there is nothing to compare with what is found
there, in the life of a flower, for those who care
Colors found in every rainbow are washed by each mornings dew
Awakened each precious day for the hungry eye to see
So love does not die

Love is like a Butterfly

Love is like the Butterfly
mostly all wings
Nourished on the nectar of nature's gift
Drawn to the beauty it has to give
Free of ownership, free of charge
Delicately patterned
Designed to draw lift and life from natures open hand
Always drawn to the beauty nature has to give
Flower to flower, face to face
Free of ownership, free of charge
a gift given to one, given to all
Never meant to be captured and held against one's will
Too tight a grip will damage what nature has woven into our lives
our wings
Too tight a grip will harm the butterfly
Tearing love and meaning from its flight
Surely love is like the butterfly
Never meant to be captured and held against its will or it will die

The Undistinguished "Close"

If it had not been for the unknown
he would have won, instead;
He came close, like so many things
Just short of the intended minimum,
The absolute, least acceptable,
The scenario moans the total
truth

But it came close, perhaps lacking in style,
limping, crawling to meet
the line
Burdened by the weight of the task
it was close!

However there is that increment
that seperates, dominates,
absolutely requires the
Forming of two distinct possibilities
of which, neither include
close

The Loser Gives More

For all the times I could have won
I had to deal with defeat
When the tally was done

To see the distorted faces
There in the crowd
And sometimes those who
screamed out loud

I stood firm and wore a grin
In spite of the hurt they shoveled in
For each champion has an easy chore
But somehow, the loser has to give more

Always There

They reach out and miss
chasing the ball
Never making the catch
yet hearing the callers call
always there the next time
They just can't stay away
Like the flower and the bee
the potter and the clay,
the lover and the loser
fate seems to have its way
Tempting those reaching out
day after day, after day

Your Father Has Died

Me and John, sisters, kids from up and down the block all in the street playing ball, roller skating, bicycles weaving in and out of the organized confusion-in and out of each other's space. The yelling of "that's not fair" or "do over", "out of my way", filled the seldom traveled street and the hot summer afternoon air.

I just finished missing the ball and my brother's utterances were less than comforting as I noticed my mother's appearance on the front porch. She looked in all directions but not at us as she started down those wooden stairs and walked directly over home plate and into the street. She had no intention of stopping. But I stopped her for a moment, my face red and sweating, dirt marks running down my cheeks. "Mom, Mom where are you going"? She barely looked down when she said, "your father died, I'm going to see my friend."

Nothing stopped, noise everywhere, "Victor, hey, Victor your turn", but the day was over. It finally happened and it went as unnoticed as a sparrow flying overhead. Nothing changed at that moment, not anything I could see or hear, but at that moment something happened that I would carry with me for the rest of my life and I knew nothing would ever be the same as I sat on the curb, no longer part of the game. I stared at my broken brown shoes, toes pointing at each other, one lace untied. "Victor, Victor get up", I could hear the yelling somewhere in a distance but I did not move, I did not look up.

I was alone, even my bully of a brother was unaware of the burden. There was no escape for either, and I knew this was something we would have to share, this time.

When I Found Out

When I found out,
my feelings took flight.

Like a wounded bird falling from the sky
I was looking for a place to rest.

Knowing, like yesterdays dreams,
I had seen my last.
And now, I feel the
things I could never
have imagined.
When I was free
of this burden.

The Hurt Will Not Go Away

When I found out it became a deafening roar

Encompassing, covering me

Like the clanging of bells or the splintered sound of cymbals

Like a thief taking all else away

Except the pain which was so real

While all else seemed so vague

Like the shadows on my wall

Like the dreams that have passed me by in an instant

No matter how hard I try

The hurt will not go away

Relentless pain, like the ocean waves searching for shore

Day after day is something I have come to endure.

Life's Garden

A pleasant day, a great time
Yet at that very same moment,
someone's hopes, someone's future is
rotting on the vine.

It started in a small milk carton,
tomato seeds...soil,
The fruit would be mine.
Given by my teacher, a joy, that just takes
time.

Somewhere in this world, I'd find a place
for this plant to grow,
It was in my Uncle's garden,
to the rear, the very last row.

It was a fine place, my father and I
agreed. Each time I went to visit
I would visit a part of me.

And with each pat of soil
my father placed about its roots,
surely he did know,
he would never taste the fruits.

At the time when seasons end,
I got to visit my plant again,
My father was gone, the garden cleared, but
my Uncle made sure, my plant was there.

In the back of the plot, it was the
very last row,
I found the place where my plant
did grow.
My thoughts were of my father gone for all
time,
As I saw my tomatoes, rotten on the vine.

A taste of sorrow, a taste of tears,
a loss clearly felt
perhaps for years.

But the plant like my father had left seeds for
tomorrow
To me this was not clear.
A small boy filled with sadness,
a small boy, filled with fears.

Changing Once and Changing Twice

When I see the storms end
I know the cycle begins again
And when I see the flowers fall
to the earth and natures call;

I know it brings new things
Like when the rooster crows or the robin sings
when the light of dawn has found
its' way
To the morning seas where
The diamonds play

Changing once and changing twice
Changing times and changing lives
Changing futures every day
He changed my life, he went away

Life's Challenge

Like a shimmering dewdrop,
Clinging to the edge of its green leafy home,
Tethered by its need to hang on;
I find myself engaging life.

One drop amongst many
Gracing a single leaf.
There in the massive sea of green
Leaves fluttering, challenging my adherence,
My grip, my determination,
My endeavor to exist there
Amongst the patch work of shapes and sizes,
Colors and reflections, expirations and demises.

Death Came By

The sun was everywhere this fine summer day
Butterflies and moths circle and play

Weeds and seeds as tall as my eye
Sitting on a curb stopped in time

Long silent moments, then a bird or a car
They seldom visit this street that doesn't go far

But today I sat and watched as death drove by
In black cars with flowers, top hats and ties

One long line for which everyone stands clear
The message like thunder as death comes near

Me as a small boy there on the curb
Holes in my shoes and the stories I've heard

Real is the death that rides slowly by,
this small boy and my blue summer sky

And I thought for a few moments between here and there
With these holes in my shoes and no procession to care

I thought what great style to be driven that way
Sitting here alone on this hot summer day

And from one of the cars a woman smiled at me
As I hid the holes in my shoes so she couldn't see

And I hid my smile as if I didn't care
Happy to be noticed I brushed back my hair

When the procession was gone and I was alone
I savored the smile the woman had shown

To this small boy on this hot day
While death and a smile came riding my way

Fire Hydrants

The fire hydrant is short and stout,
Built close to the ground,
Fully dressed in reds and yellows
It's shaped round and round

Seeming to be all alone,
Singular, never a pair,
Yet an iron sea of networks there

When the summer is hot
They can make it cool
It's Johnny's jump on the way to school

Sometimes first base, second or third
There on a city block
Where I threw my first curve
The iron man, domed hat, arms outstretched,
showering the kids, dogs, and other pets.

But at 9:00 P.M. every night
and sometimes ten
Mister James and his dog visit and visit again
And in those dark shadows
Johnnie pissed out his beer,
Put out his cigarette and left it there.

To some a place to sit,
Waiting at the curb

To some invisible,
A fixture, never heard

It's so easy to forget
To consider naught,
Yet even a fire hydrant
Deserves some special thought.

Alone

In the beginning there was an irreversible sadness. There was a great loss, and the reality of being alone, at least, where ones feelings of security and comfort are concerned. Father was gone. The knowledge that this part is over and things will not continue as they are, which frightened and saddened me. I was sitting on the back stairs, looking beyond the Weeping Willow tree, the yard, and over the brook that incited fear and recreation. I watched the Mintorie's car sway and bounce as they drove away and I knew they would not return.

I knew once again I would miss them even though "Red Head Mintori" would steal cooling pudding or pies off the backyard second story porch leaving me, and my brothers and sisters, wanting for what was lost.

I felt a great emptiness forever when I remembered that day. Or the time "Money Bags", a small negro man and his friends shared a bottle on a cold December night while spray painting an old car, keeping warm with their familiar open fire that licked at the vapors until the whole world turned to fire. One poor fellow came to rest in the corner down on his knees, hands fixed in prayer position. I hope he found his God. Money Bags survived, strained gait, alone in his mottled world as he crept along forever after.

Sour Syrup

The free wielding hand of time and death intruded
And carved out a chunk of life
Taking away that which was mine
Like an awesome, tireless knife

Carving and changing the landscape
Changing songs and changing rhymes
Changing smiles and changing faces
Creating endless holes, endless lines

Pouring life into darkness
Like the sour syrup of time
Haunting all that choose to live
With its endless command of time.

In Bed Midnight

The tree branches scratched at the window pane
Like an unwanted visitor in the night
While I lie in my bed, darkened room
Fatherless boy filled with fright

Frosted panes like ghostly stains
Separate me from the howling winds
As the frozen persistence of winters rage
Hold me captive here within

Scratching, scratching as though begging entry,
Like fingers reaching from trees
The cold persistent shadows mixed with light
Creep through the window touching me.

Void of feeling these jagged patterns
Come dancing on my face and hands
Reaching through from frozen world
Frightening this young man.

Day to Day

I love to dream and escape the theme
So many frightened people live day to day
I lose my cares and silly fears
I dream and dream away

I watch the sky and shapes drift by
As the sun just shines away
I hum a song I haven't known long
In a world of frightening gray

The Housing Projects

There were the housing projects, Bishop Walsh, twelve red brick mountains dotted with windows that appeared like hollow openings, entry to another world, and they were. The buildings were surrounded by grass which was bordered by short posts connected by chains that were intended to keep all away from the grass. A few young trees stood alone like flag poles without flags in this river valley. Some of the river survived the test of time, flowing free but soiled. It was home to foul smelling things, dead things, living things, balls and bottles, paint cans and things unrecognizable. Even so it was a playground, a museum that had a ragged patch of meadow on its' border. Some would see it as an abandoned lot, but I saw it as a meadow. On the river bank I saw shapes and geometries, toys and a world far from the boredom that stalked its' victims, there beyond the highway which separated these worlds.

The highway also took lives like the time both of my sisters were hit by a car while crossing to reach a store on the other side, but they survived. I was a nine year old who braved it almost daily without incident to reach my world of freedom. There I found blue sky, free flowing water and a peace in being alone in a part of the world I could call my own.

In the belly of the valley, the ancient river reduced in size, soiled by the world around it, still flowed to the ocean, clinging to life like so many across the highway living and dying in their own ways. Captured in the tall brick buildings which almost all hoped to escape and flow free beyond the valley into a world that looked down on them from the ridge line above. It seemed as though even the people in fast moving cars wanted to get away from that which surrounded them as they passed through the valley like a train, day after day.

The River

As a young boy
Perhaps nine or ten
Feeling quite solemn
Alone without friends

Looked for a place
To feel at home
To find the things
That hadn't gone wrong

There in the grass
Rose the rocky shore
To guide the jewel
That I adore

There to the rocks
My body conformed
Watching the glimmer
The tides adorned

As it flowed by
The birds came in
I sat to watch
Mans greatest friend

And the river flowed
Left and sometimes right
In the morning sun
And returned at night

And I always knew
As ships went by
They would return
On the evening tide

And as the water
Rose and fell
I knew the world
Was doing quite well

And sitting here is, proof I see
The river flows forever
With silent speed

And I'm not alone
On an empty shore
I have found peace
Flowing and pure.

The Rivers Gifts

As a boy I had few toys
To play the games with other boys
So I found a place to spend the day
There by the river I dreamt and played

The tide would bring such simple joys
Like bottles and balls to this small boy
And when a can would float my way
I'd pry the lid and paint the day

I'd dig the banks along the shore
To find a coin for this small boy
For those that knew or chose to assess
It was no place for a boy, a sewer at best

But amongst the discarded, the rocks and soil,
I found a place you could not spoil

When the tugs and their barges pushed on by
Sometimes I waved, sometimes I smiled
I often skipped rocks to pass the day
Or watch the sea birds dive stray

And on those days when I made a fire
I'd roast a potato or strip copper wire

Each time the tide claimed the shore
I knew tomorrow it would bring much more

Of all toys the river brought to me
It brought a place where I was free

Water Runs Free

The water runs free, shimmering, changing itself with color and
motion
Graced by displays of uncut diamonds that jump and skip along the
surface
like flying fish on the move

Here where I sit I am bathed in quiet, silence, like the night birds flight
across the moonlit sky, or the breeze that graces my skin, cooling that
which is warmed by the sun

There is a subtle greatness found in being alone and at peace with that
which
flows free, filling my world with beauty, free flowing gifts
that so few will ever know or seldom see

Birds

Birds, birds, they've seen the world
I watch them circle, I watch them swirl
I've seen them pattern,
I've seen them glide
High above my spirits fly

Looking at the Sky

I looked up today and I saw the sky in an unusual way
The same sky that is always there, but today unusually bright,
unusually clear
Sitting here, nestled alone, in a sunny spot where the grass had grown
A cluster of starling on the wing, a change of direction and back again
Black pointed patterns against the blue sky
Performing undaunted, performing up high
I saw the sky in an unusual way
I saw it when I looked up today!

Iron Bound

With cold hard reasoning, no mercy for those who need it, I carried on amongst the teenage maze, houses and alleys, alleys and houses, narrow streets. I became part of what it does to people, the young, the old, the ones who carry on and the lost souls. This part of the city seemed to be without bright color or sun, a brown, burnt orange and gray landscape well adapted to its formal name, the Iron Bound Section or even the informal moniker "Down Neck". The names came from its one time industrial base and its geography. The names mirrored its attitudes and vulnerabilities reflected in the violence and misguided emotions that required almost daily confrontations of one form or another.

Of course there were the moments of laughter like the tours given by my next door neighbor, short red headed Bobby or "Bubbles" as he was called. Almost everyone had a nickname. Bubbles was a friendly kid respected by none, asked for very little yet gave as much as he could.

One thing he gave was a tour of the neighborhood for his newly arrived neighbor which included a visit with the "bums" that lived under the skyway. There were liberties that came with the knowledge of the secret dark holes scattered about like carnival rides. Bubbles especially enjoyed a trip to the rail yard where swine were parked waiting to be carried off for the slaughter. He called them "Oinkers". I was surprised to see their huge size and how tightly they were packed into the wooden slatted rail cars, their uneasiness when we approached and the layer of urine and fecal matter that the Oinkers stood in. It must have been six inches deep. Their black eyes peered through the slats and watched us as we walked alongside the filthy foul smelling cargo, listening to their squeals and uneasy jockeying for room where there was none.

Bubbles said, "Hey Victor watch this" as he picked up a long pointed stick and began to probe between the slats finding the ribs of the frozen in place swine. As we walked along he poked and prodded laughing at the squeals of the doomed when he saw a rare opportunity emerge. The one thing that escaped the confines of that filthy world and into the sunlight, other than the squeals, was the ear of a poor beast. The ear lay against the wooden slat, a sorry symbol of the only freedom granted to this parade of madness. Once again, "hey Victor, watch this". Bubbles moved up cautiously as not to disturb the unwitting victim and perhaps see his target withdraw back into the hell from which it came.

Raising the stick above his head in the noon day sun and coming down with a well aimed blow, the "Oinker" screamed, his scream followed by a rumbling sound from within and a huge guffaw by Bubbles. At that very moment the creature's foot stomped down into the sea of filth and sent a squirt of this vile substance through the slats to find the open mouth of his tormentor and painted his freckled face. I laughed in amusement as Bubble's reward for a job well done was expelled in a choking fashion as he briskly rubbed the streaks from his face by lifting his tee shirt off his stomach and wiping furiously.

Bubbles suddenly lost interest in the stock yard and quickly scurried across the tracks under the skyway down a long street that flowed into a meadow. That magnificent meadow had reeds rolling like a sea of beige water. On either side of the entry rose a forest of huge sunflowers, eight foot tall stalks with pods as large as my chest, surrounded by bright yellow petals standing like brightly colored guards to this magnificent world. This was something I had never seen before, a sunflower. Something within me was awakened as I stared up in utter disbelief at what stood before me and the meadow that beckoned with its watery bay just beyond.

I found some kind of peace, some kind of home beyond the stock yards, beyond the rails, beyond my young companion, who did not see nor understand what had just filled my world.

Even though I desperately wanted to touch these magnificent pods, examine and feel their texture, I could not bring myself to pull one down. In some strange way I felt they were greater than my curiosity, greater than all I had seen that day. I made little mention to my companion, for fear even this would be laid to waste. I entered the meadow and disappeared among the reeds.

Reed Instrument

The wind rushed through the meadow
Tugging at the reeds making patterns of yellow and brown
While it whistled through my clothing
Filling me with sound
Playing me like a reed instrument
Fluttering, fluttering, pin wheel round and round

Standing there part of the natural sound
Orchestra of natures' components
Natures colors, feelings and pictures
Me an instrument, in the meadow I've found

Winter Meadow

The cold frosty silence reached out across the meadow like a white
blanket.
It covered the rushes, the motion, the whispers, and the call of the lark,
the chatter filled summer days
I once knew.
Now like a mirror the unblemished white crystals were home to sun
filled arrays flickering and swirling
along the surface
They stop and cling to the feather tipped reeds that reach up through
the snow so as not to be
forgotten.
They stand captured by winters' grand statement, frozen in time, for
wandering eye to see.
Peering between blackened trees reaching up like out stretched arms
holding all in place, separating
road from meadow, meadow from rail.
Lacing all with blue black shadows that meander across the surface
captured by the moan of winters'
angry chilling winds which none can escape.
Not even the small black specks that arrive on the wing to pattern and
dot the landscape, moving
about like strangers walking in circles, searching for lost valuables.
Above all there seems to be a freedom as grand and as acceptable as
the summer world I knew, which
in time, will reclaim its' command of the landscape.

Me and my Peers

As I sit here all alone
I think of the moments from
which I have grown

And all the choices I had
back then
Unknown to me and my many friends

It kept me short when I could have
gone long
Undecided when I could have
grown strong

Unhappy when the joys were
there
Such sorry boys; me and my peers

Charlie's Rose

A tough place
Showered me with scars and memories
I can't erase

A port town
A section called "Down Neck"
I joined the crowd
What the heck

There was Charlie
Lived next door
Fifty years old
or more

Two kids, bright red hair,
A drinking wife, who did not care

Nothing much good grew down there
just mad men, bad men
coercion and fear

Patterns of shadows and green
Rows of fences set between

Yards of dirt all set in a row
Charlie wanted roses
Why, I don't know

He lived all winter with a mail order dream
Pictures of roses were all he could see

Thorny short branches came in a box
Brought by the postman

To his dirt lot

Charlie on his knees
Holes in a row
Dreaming of roses
He hoped would grow

There were times he looked for them in a bottle
This poor working class man
Hands chipped and mottled
But these roses would be so grand

He had a dog, Nipper, both black and white
Moving amongst the shadows
He looked silver in the moon's generous light

We saw Nipper approach the rose bushes
While still without a flower
And Nipper did what dogs would do
There in the midnight hour

My brother and I stood and watched
Nipper do what he would do
It caused both to laugh out loud
Then we pissed on the roses too

There in the maze of streets and yards
People and poison
going too far

I stood in the moonlight
Just a young boy
Without really knowing
What I helped to destroy

Memories

Memories are a part of us all
They are a moonlit night or a ravens call
A cool drink on a hot summer's day
Or a gnawing pain that won't go away

Memories, the things we made
A frosted glass or colored vase
Opened topped cars and summer fun
Loves and losses wars and guns

Memories are smiles and frowns
Deadly, seriously, painted clowns
Reds and greens, Christmas and such
Sadness and despair darkness and dust

Temptation

The sun had fallen and the soft orange lights began to fill the avenue. The diner across the street started to throw its shadows on the sidewalk and the cars idled while waiting for the light to change. You could smell them. You could hear them. You could almost reach out and touch them, as they stopped to buy an Evening News from the short fat cigar toting peddler who took up residence in front of the bank, when the sun went down. I was the kid sitting on the bank steps waiting for the crowd to gather as it did every night in the summer. Soon there would be a flood of wise guys cursing, pushing and pulling, challenges and challenges.

I looked up and there was Sophie, pretty young girl dressed in tight white pants and loose blouse. "Hey! Victor", she smiled from ear to ear, displaying her bright white teeth. "All alone"? Stating the obvious, "come on, make room" as she dropped herself in my lap and wiggled around. The perfume filled my senses and her warm soft body filled my lap. This was Junior's girl but at that moment she availed to me that which frightened me most. That which could capture me, take hold of my senses for the moments of pleasure and cut off my way out of this neighborhood.

This temptation was gently placed here in my lap. I hoped it did not cost me one of the very few luxuries left to me, my freedom, and the desire to leave this place. So, for a moment, I unsuccessfully tried to ignore that which I could not ignore, finally reasoning that her young body was much stronger than mine. I realized she would win all contests of will.

The Smile

The warm intense smile
Something I will never forget
Called to me like I had never known
Surely there was magic upon her face
In the smile she had shown
And for all the fears and indecision
That come creeping in subtle tones
I freed myself to make the acquaintance
No longer was I alone

A Dream of Love

It would be forever she whispered.
And the shades of love that shone upon
Her face, were her escape from the
truth

The beads of sweat upon our bodies
appeared as tears for me.
She lay still, I could feel her
warmth and her softness nestled
in our calm

I could feel her dream of love, and
it saddened me
Tomorrow, and yet Tomorrow, might
it ever be the same

Something New

There she was, fine flesh
Waving that temptation like Old Glory
on the Fourth of July
The crowd went wild to see such beauty
and she went wild for such a crowd
She somehow lost herself that day or,
maybe she found something new,
I just don't know.

It's taken fifty two years and I find myself here,
looking back at all the fools I've known,
Scattered along the roadside, broken and destroyed
by something they once called new.
Yet the romance only lasted so long,
and the new soon became old, even dangerous,
like walking in traffic.
Blinded and seduced by new things, yesterday became final,
she was gone forever.

Lost Romance

She was so dazzling, so fancy
Such fun to be with
So ripe for romancing
I watched her move in and out
Around and around all about
But I lost sight of her
Like a river that flows around a bend
Driven by all that is behind
Shimmering and sparkling in the sunlight

In that distant place that hides all
Beyond the trees, around the bend
I lost a treasured love
To the same passions that brought her to me
My world, my loss
Filled with knowing and regretting
This river became part of the oceans
and ultimately a memory in the endless sea of memories

When She Looks Back

When I asked her if she loved
me so
She said the answer she did not
know

And I put my head down
So I did not see her frown
And I searched for something
more to say

During that pause
she reflected my flaws

And her love was held at bay.

And the angry seas where lovers grieve
swelled up that stormy day
The rising tide engulfed
my pride.

I wept in solitary dismay

So we parted and when she
walked from view
She created a memory for her future too!
Now when she looks back
I won't be there
Just the memory and how
much I cared

The Moth

Like the moth that flickers, flits
About the candles flame

I was consumed by the romance

Darting and dashing
Moving in, flirting, taunted
By the beauty
Blinded with the obsession

Condemned by all that is
Frightened by the fire
Captured and inspired

And the candle flickered on
Moth after moth

Mickey

My thoughts drifted to Mickey. Someone I would never forget. Ragged derelict sleeping under the skyway on cardboard ,always a sad figure, his clothes wrinkled and torn, his appearance like a piece of paper rolled in a ball and then out- stretched so that he appeared as a kind of jagged, odd geometry.

He didn't seem to struggle to survive, he just took what came his way as though he were a pane of glass and life, like so many rain drops, just beat against him. He had a pointed nose, sitting on furrowed face, hair hanging down, dirty and brown, with a memory of blonde thrown in. Mickey would sometimes appear when he needed a drink but was unable to gather fifty cents for a cheap bottle of chemicals the Gallo Brothers, Earnest and Julio, marketed as wine. The taste was something only the desperate would hunt for. Its long term effect had long since taken hold of Mickey and the taste was merely a comma in the harsh sentence it would impose on any of its followers.

This night Mickey greeted me but something additionally wretched had placed its burden on him. It saddened me to see such misery. This empty shell of a man had his face cut, nose broken but the bleeding had stopped, the swelling and bruising jumped out and grabbed me like one of those neon signs that filled the avenue. Mickey did not know my name, he had no need of names but I knew his. "Mick what happened, Jesus what happened?" I was very familiar with the violence down here and expected some had befallen this wretched creature. Mick sat down and replied softly, "the DTs". "The DTs?, what the hell is that Mick?" Mick hesitated and said, "That's what happens when I can't get a drink." I hesitated, it still did not make sense. "What the hell are you talking about?" "Not having a drink can't do that to you!" Mick replied, "when you live like I do, it does." He continued on, "I drink so much that when I stop, I lose control, it's called Delirious Tremors, that's what happened." I looked at him searchingly, "but your face Mick?" " That, oh that happened, I guess, I must have fallen, don't know." "I had never heard of this before. Mick, how long has this been going on?" " For a long time, buddy, for a long time." He shook his head and stared down at his hands. Beneath the blood and dirt stains there were some tattoos on his fingers. "The worst part was those damn Germans" he said. "I could feel them bayoneting me, screaming, beating me, they were all around me. I felt all the pain as though it was really happening. That's what the DTS are like." " What Germans, Mick?" It was almost twenty three years since the war started and about eighteen since it ended. I knew this because I always heard talk of WW2 and it grabbed my interest. I said it again, "why Germans, Mick?" Mick sheepishly looked at me, then down at his clasped hands, then down at his shoes. He stared away and said, "I was in the Navy. " "Yeah, go on", I replied. "During the war," Mick said, looking around. "Oh a lot of guys were, my Uncle was in the Army fighting the Japs." " Are you saying that's what did it?" "Kind of", Mick replied.

At that moment I felt Mick was a bum feeling sorry for himself. There were a lot of them under the skyway, living in the flop houses along Market Street, lined up at the blood bank on McCarter Highway. That was a place that truly earned the name blood money. Mick must have sensed my uneasiness with such an excuse. He continued on. "We were out in the Atlantic, our ship was hit and it went down fast, some of us survived, a dozen or so, and were left floating, the rest went down with the ship, many went down with the ship." "So how did you make it back?", I asked. Mick looked at his hands again and quietly said, "the German sub came up. They said they wanted two volunteers to work, all others would be left to their fate". Tears came to his eyes and he said, "no one volunteered except me and another guy." "I never saw the other guy again after going with the Germans".

I didn't ask about the remaining sailors in the water as I was starting to feel Mick's pain. "What did they make you do?" If one could grow more sullen, Mick did. "They made me work in the bottom of the ship, in the engine room, a bad place". "Were they as mean as they say?"I asked. "Some were miserable, some were alright, I guess, but I was not treated well." "How did you talk to them?" "I learned to speak German", he replied. "How long were you with them?" "Three years", he replied. "You were in the bottom of the boat for three years?" "Mostly", he said, "except for going back to Germany a couple of times.

I was taken off the boat a few times when they started to trust me."
"Why?" I wanted to know. "Where would I go?" Mick replied, "I never
knew where I was."

Mick opened his hands palms down and on each finger there were
tattoos that were undistinguishable. "See those" he uttered, "they
were Swastikas" and he pulled up his sleeve and there were more odd
shaped tattoos." Did they do that to you, Mick?" "No", he said quietly,
"I did it hoping they would stop being mean to me." His voice broke
and he almost began to cry. "I became one of them or tried to be.
Every time I go into these DTs they come back."

I began to believe what I was being told and felt for this bloodied
torn man. "Mick", I said softly, "Mick how did you get back?" "One night
they came to me and said they needed my help. Somehow, somewhere,
I didn't know where I was, they needed my American voice to arrange
an oil pick up. Nothing much was explained but the sub surfaced and
three of us got into a raft and paddled ashore."

"As soon as my feet hit the sand, I started to run and I didn't look
back. I didn't know where I was or even who I was. The military record
would show I was lost at sea. If I appeared and claimed my identity,
I would probably be shot." "I found out I was in New Jersey, Asbury
Park. I covered the tattoos as best I could and became a nobody, a
drunk, a dead man."

I knew if some of my friends heard about this they would not be
kind. So I never repeated it, but it made no difference, once again
Mickey vanished. I never saw him again. Yet every time I look back,
there is Mick's marker etched into my memory.

The Ocean's Secrets

The sea came in to greet us
We sat perched on silver sand

The gulls encircled our consciousness
Waiting for helping hand

The bathers jumping and leaping
Like dolphins of the land

The rushing of the water
Like the pounding of a band

Here we sit in summer breeze
Perched on silver sand

Who knows what lies out there
Beyond the foaming shore

The fisherman and the sailor
And those who are no more
The nameless wrecks and secrets kept
From all they once adored

Far below a world I know
There on ocean floor

And the terns turn as widows
Yearn
For those they will see no more

Far below where some things go
As the oceans slams its door

Yet I must admit
From where I sit
It all seems so grand

Safe and secure on oceans shore
Perched on silver sand

Looking Back

When I sit and remember the scheme
There behind me seldom seen

I feel the feelings I felt back then
I know the price that I didn't know when

And looking back at the world
Scattered behind me, flags unfurled

Sometimes banners and sometimes none
Sometimes death, and sometimes fun

So paint me sorry or paint me grey
Paint me January, but paint me May

And each time I feel the season end
I feel the feelings I felt back then

And sometimes alone, I know that's true
When I'm looking back as I sometimes do

Drunken Rant

So now that I'm drunk
I can rhyme the word, forsake the cliche and write
the absurd

How total is total
How final is dust
How much can I take
Before I must

Some of these things
I've never known
How happy is happy
How home is home

How truly is truth
How few is none
How sad is your life
when the life is done

Come to me sweet tomorrow
Like a high flying bird
I'll taunt you with your madness
I'll sample your absurd

I'll fill the air with sadness
I'll fill the heart with rhyme
I'll fill the morn with each
child that's born
I'll plant your seeds and mine

So what of the brew
The ages stewed
To mix its blood with mine
and who'd ever think
That just a few drinks
Can make me feel just fine

Life By Chance

How little is too little
When the counting is done
Once I had plenty
Now I have none

Once I had a full boat
To brave the angry seas
Against the tide, my spirits high
Not afraid to bleed

But life can be cruel, and by chance,
A flurry of burdens I did see
So I pounded and toiled and sometimes spoiled
even that which was good to me.

The Traveler

Distant faces passed by night,
In the many small towns I've known
The miles of road and rails behind
Are the memories of being alone

With shirttails flapping in the wind
I've more than lived a life,
And each time I look behind
I've traveled that distance twice

The sound of mugs and the smell of ale,
A barroom clogged with smoke,
Splintered cheers and sorrowful sneers
We enjoy another bad joke

Cracked walls yellow with smoke
Meet a ceiling, it's color I could not tell
And above the roar of a drunken whore
I could hear the barkeeps yell

I'll have one more for no good reason
A habit and a friend
To face the cold against my cheek
Back on the road again

The moan of a distant freight
Covers blackened fields on either side
My footsteps point to the clatter
I have a place to ride

A ride past whispering voices
Heard through towering trees
Past a world of golden sunsets
A parade of Autumn leaves

And down below the rails
They sing of sweet home
I sit and hum a tune
But I sit and hum alone

Sometimes empty barns or traveler's yarns
I smile at the stories I'm told
Coffee and hay at the end of a day
For a man that's tired weary and cold

Yet I watch the spring flowers bloom
I feel the earth grow moist beneath my feet
And upon my back, the sun
A warm gentle treat

I've seen the summers come,
And the arrival of the first Autumn leaf
I've felt the winters angry chill
Sometimes breathless, magnificent, a thief

The city lights, sounds and sights,
The once familiar place I called home
I left them all behind
For a chance to travel alone

Sunday Mornings

I was coming out of Margie's Corner store on Elm and Pulaski, newspaper in hand. It was a Sunday morning moving toward another mid-day Down Neck, shadows falling on one side of the street while the other side was lit up by the rising sun. A time when some were coming home from church, it seemed like there was a church every other block. I never went, it was foreign to me. I remembered what happened to Barbara when she went to Father Smith for help and I knew then this was not for me. When my father was alive, I and my brothers and sisters had to go, every Sunday. My father did not know Barbara. This was the time when coming home from church meant carrying a white box filled with buns from the bakery, long white bags following the shape of the Italian bread. That bread would traditionally have the end torn off not long after being placed on the kitchen table. This time it had been delivered untouched as mom wanted it. As soon as she examined it and turned her back someone always tore off the end and dipped it into her simmering gravy. She always expected it, yet always acted surprised and scolded the one she caught. She really never wanted to stop the tradition; it was testament to the taste and value of her gravy. She would often let me sample because I always asked permission, that was the kind of kid I was and she knew otherwise I would never partake in the privilege.

But this morning, down below in the narrow street, narrow minds in large cars were headed on a collision course. One turning west and the other doing the same into a single lane street until neither one could move. Screams and insistence filled the air but these brutes were an even match when it came to this sort of thing. One monster thought a baseball bat would settle who went first, while the other knew a pistol of large caliber would be the deciding factor and he was correct. Both had wives and children aboard to witness their determination, their command of the situation, and I knew either one was bound by honor to back up his threat. I had seen this before but this was the worst.

One woman had to watch her husband die on an otherwise quiet Sunday morning, and one witnessed her husband throw away everything they had when the bullet met its' target. One bully found eternity and the other a prison cell. Neither place had white boxes filled with jelly or cream donuts, or a pot of gravy for dipping bread. I walked up Elm Street my back to the blood stained street and the cries of women in terror who had lost all they had on this day, on this small street, for some small reason.

I wondered what the future would bring for me.

The Fox

Life has been unusual for me
Good and bad at the same time
I know I must choose my passion
As I must choose my wine

Circling, Circling, all the time

Like the wily fox so seldom seen
Hiding from the hunter, to and fro
and in between
Keeping a safe distance from the fracas
the confusion, the unbalanced scene

I don't know whether I should be grateful or frightened
by some of the things I've seen

The Bully

It came to me in a whisper
Mournful in hushed tones
Like the unspoken at a funeral
The one who sits alone

Today it was his choice
And I was the intended victim at hand
So I took the life with my favorite knife
And about my shoes ran the blood of this man.

And it came to me in a whisper
Now that the killing was done,
For there was a chance in this murderous dance
That I would be the one.

And for the reasons of a few
I do what I do
To those who impose on me,
So I plunged the knife into the life
Of the fool who wouldn't let it be.

Dark was the night, as dark as the deed
And regretfully I was the one
To take this hulk and retire his bulk
While he was just having fun.

There was a time when I might beg,
A time when I might plead
Before I knew what I had to do
To bring him to his knees.

Blood upon my face,
The feeling of sticky, on my hands,
Now etched deep into my memory,
The death of another man.

And for each one that kills
He kills something of his own
He took some of my life as he accepted the knife
While his blood soaked through my clothes.

It came to me in a whisper,
Mournful in hushed tones,
He could have been as he was then;
If he had only left me alone.

The Front

I knew of a
restaurant
On the down side of downtown

And things weren't always
As they looked
Like things hiding in a jungle,
Or the cover of a book

Like painting glorious
Pictures
Over a picture of fear

I learned to be an
Artist
Amongst the checkered
Table clothes
And half drunk glasses of
beer

Seven Stories High

I began to think of the life I took,
How easy it was done,
With no second look

and way up here on the seventh floor,
outside my window,
a seed grows once more

And here on a sill no dirt
or soil
A small crack beckoned a seed,
to life they were so loyal

And in that obscure place
dancing on a sill
Life was springing from death
as life often will

Just beyond my reach I watched
it grow
So frail so desperate
And so all alone

Up here in my isolation
with the thing I had done
Sometimes there was a bird
but a flower only one

And for all the winds
and all the times,
this seed came to live
where death seems to thrive

With all the terrible memories
buried within these walls
Just outside my window
a single flower grows.

It was not dramatic in its shape or form
Just a small purple flower;
The stem had some thorns

And I thought of the life I took
How easy it was done
With no second looks

And I ask myself why a single seed climbs seven stories
and finds a crack to survive

I took a life when I had the time
I took away the gift
no care, no mind.

Day by day I pay the cost
No taste for the gift
the other had lost

So be it flower
I know you will die
Once again I'll be left alone
Seven stories high

The Hanging

A chill raced down his spine
As he sat in suit of shabby gray
Knowing there before him
Was the price he'd have to pay

Others had gone before him
On and off the platforms at hand
But he is left choice less and weary
Death awaits this marked man

Once with locks golden blonde
He sailed kites across Everett's Field
And sat in rugs of endless green
When life was all but real

He dreamed he'd sail on endlessly
Just him his kite and dreams
Master of his own fanciful fortunes
His hopes and endless schemes

Now a butcher, a baker, a schoolmarm
All watching from distant shore
Face good, bad, some even sad
And some from behind church door

His knees seemed to falter
Yet he rose to accept his fate
Eyes were peered and throats were cleared
As he assumed a pompous gait

His last chore a simple one
Make this spectator's day
To allow them to look upon his face
As he looked upon that of his prey

His mother, his dear sweet mother
Thank God she was spared this day
For he should die his own death
And kill no more in his murderous way

The crowd seemed uneasy, muffled
Even humbled to witness death
No pain, no sorrow, no regret
Awaiting his last dying breath

The platform seemed much higher now
As his footsteps echoed against wooden stand
The air was clear the sound precise
May all take note, this is a marked man

The breeze licked at his shirttails
As he looked hungrily at the sky
Nature had given it's last gift
To a man condemned to die

The executioner found his mark
His cold fingers danced hungrily about the chin
His last gaze about the countryside
Seemed to produce a somewhat forgotten grin

With black silken hood placed about his head
He could feel the heat of his own breath
While all about him he could hear them rising
Rising to the tune of death

The reader read his own words of death
A pause, might the whole world take a bow
All seemed so distant, so gray
Then shocking tumultuous, loud

Once with locks golden blonde
He sailed kites across Everett's Field
And sat in rugs of endless green
When life was all but real

Give and Take

I have tried to understand
The many faces that some people show
Sometimes three different people
In the one person I know
Rolling out ones madness
Like the baker rolls out his dough

So determined and driven
No matter what may be
Desires and imbalance
In the madness I see
Like the market where all is stolen
Until the merchant ceases to be

Till the lush greens have withered
Where an oasis filled a need
Till the garden is no more
And the fruit has gone to seed
Till everything has disappeared
The difference between them and me

I Wear it Like a Rose

Have you ever walked a cornfield
In the early spring morn

Have you ever held a Robin's egg
Before the Robin's born

Have you ever nurtured the small ones
Or chased a high flying ball
Or walked away in silence
When you didn't like the call

Have you ever known humility
or worn it like a rose
Or walked away from something awful
all the others chose

Have you ever hoped for tomorrow
and found it didn't come true
But kept on hoping
and tried to see it through

Have you ever appreciated sadness
as mourners sometimes do?
Or pressed the flowers to the casket
of someone close to you

Have you ever dealt with madness
and the things that madmen do
Or the wild eye and stark surprise
when the madness comes peering through

Or love the place;
Or love the time;
Or love the poet
Or love his rhyme

Have you ever been left standing there
When everyone else had gone home
Or continued to give till there
was no more
Then found yourself alone

Have you ever found none
Where you thought something should be
or given away your best
for x,y.and z

Have you ever been fooled
when you were absolutely sure,
or counted three
when there were actually four

Thought it was high
But it was really low
Thought it was useless
When it wasn't so

Have you ever had a love
That you just couldn't let go
Or a favorite thing that;
Just hurt you so

Have you ever recognized, that,
which others seldom see
or lost your place in line
because you couldn't let it be.

Like tripping on a stair
Like falling from a tree
Coming back to Earth
Was never easy for me

Flickering Lives

All alone and searching
Bankrupt memories like
empty hotels
Finding no place with
comfort
In a darkened prison cell

There across the courtyard
Those cigarettes flicker from window
sills
And skeletons dance
a prison dance
In every prison cell

And tonight is no different
from any that I have known
There amongst the darkness
the flicker and the bones

You just can feel the madness
Its signs are everywhere
There amongst the
darkness
The flickers and despair

And every night there comes
these lights
As the darkness closes in
It compresses my world
To the flickers and swirls
And the fate of these
desperate men.

Prisoner Torment

So sad this life I've had.

Empty pockets, no steady dad
No loving mother or summer fun
No smile on my face where the
misery was hung

And most would never know
the hole in my shoe where the
weather goes

Such an insidious thing
So many kinds of being alone
The familiar thread of angry dread
Have built this prison home

And the prison sounds heard at night
Comfort the dead and steal the life
They rattle the bones of those who care
And echo tomorrow for those who dare

They challenge the hope of those who survive
And frighten the forsaken where the loneliness
thrives

Alone at Midnight

Sitting alone, darkness,
cigarette flickering
A lighthouse in the vastness of being
Acrid smoke clinging
Surrounding me and my thoughts
Preying on my senses
Remnants of old memories
Haunting the darkness
Here all alone.

A light flickering
There in the darkness
Over and over again
Bearer of lost dreams
In endless sea
My solemn universe
Where all that appears alive
is the cigarette
That flickers and clings to me
like madness
Fashioned in the midnight hour

Too Late to Change the Deal

Now I sit and wonder why
Although much too late to change a guy

I feel the fears of growing old
Yet still confused as I've been told

Lost loves I could have known
Traded for naught, fears overgrown

Living without what others may feel
And it's kind of late to change the deal

I don't know how it all went wrong
But I'm left here to hum a somber song

Seems no difference who I meet
This tired old man is seldom sweet

This wrinkled face shows the pain
Like furrowed earth worn by rain

The weary times I spent alone
In a darkened room I once called home

Wandering through me most every day
Ghosts and regrets have their way

These are the things I often feel
But it's kind of late to change the deal

Choice

Choice is the burden as deep as the sea
Sometimes it's you and sometimes it's me

Sometimes I fight and sometimes I flee
Sometimes I forget just how powerful a choice can be

The Orange Light

A dim orange invades his prison cell each night, casting shadows on
the walls
casting shadows on dying men
Casting shadows on faceless names and places scratched into the wall
Scratched into everyone's life that enters this world
Stark reminders of so many misguided deeds
paid for by each breath they breathe
Life stealing time over and over again since who knows when
sitting alone in a cell amongst many
His thoughts churned and tossed like small boat on angry sea
while the dim orange light fills the nights and colors everything he
sees
He sits alone, silent, motionless staring down at his shoes
although there is nothing to see just shoes and sad memories
Shoes and memories that go nowhere beyond this six by ten for so
many lost and broken men
Surely tomorrow night, like every night, the dim orange light will
return again

I Don't Know If I Can Take It Anymore

And I wondered if I could take it
anymore

As my emotions poured out and
lie quivering on the floor

For all the emotion, the exhausting
push and pull

The gains and the losses,
the silks and the wools

The bridals and the brides we all
came to know

The passionate lover, the rain
and the snow
The moments that seemed so heavy
the rushing to the door

I feel saddened by the nagging
question

Can I take this anymore?

I Remember Julie

There were the teenage years, the growing up, all the fears, sex, misunderstanding and brutality practiced in this port town. Newark, New Jersey, with all its misery, fine trappings, dirty streets, crumbling black neighborhoods, Italian ghettos, fine Forest Hills and Weequahic Sections.

Italians, Jews, Blacks, Irish, Polish and Germans at war, eager to capture a part of something they could claim.

There was the forfeiture of family and the blind searching for romance with empty pockets, empty soul.

There was a yearning for all that was out of reach to a young man.

Love was something I did not understand and was afraid of. An abstract emotion that drew me closer, not knowing what it might do to me or to those I would come to know.

All these things flowing into the brutality so close to me and my involvement, fostered the fear that I would be devoured by that which swirled around me.

I will always remember Julie. A girl with braces and short cropped hair that was used by every animal she ever went near. They searched for her and she was never safe. I felt her pain, her life, which the animals could not see. She was a poor girl with high I.Q. I knew her in grammar school, in the corner store, in those familiar tormented moments. There amongst what we were born into, amongst the things so deadly present yet most couldn't see. I still feel for her and now wonder if she remembers me.

It was a world of lost hopes and children. Drugs running through the city like a torrent of streams leaving sores on all that it touched with a velocity that pulled in all that was stagnant or near its fast running current of muddy water, garbage and the things that drugs help you to forget as they bury you.

I met those who had taken a life, maybe a few, those who destroyed all they touched. They destroyed folks like me, folks like you. I felt love was beyond my grasp, my borders, and the people I knew. There was this great hollow feeling, the empty barrel that rolls down hill with people moving aside as people will. I could never truly reach out until the barrel stood still.

Love

Love is the fruit that grows on the best of trees
Love is what would always soothe
when we fell and skinned our knees

Love was that shiny new bike,
the strong winds that flapped the tails and filled the sails
it helped me fly my kite

Love was the mother that held me close
Brushed back my hair, to see my eyes,
to see my smile, which she liked most

Time exposes loves many sides as the shattered pane of glass
Resting on floor, spread about, separate from the whole
Never to return to once a single mass

Love has never again been so simple as when I was young
It seems to change and sometimes grow
into the sighs and the sadness I've come to know

Rewards to Woes

Round and round the cycle goes
Top to bottom rewards to woes
Something in and something out
Planted nothing and here's a sprout

Earth and sky, water and sand
I released my catch I caught by hand
I forgave all loves that wouldn't stick
Could find no candle with infinite wick

There is no love you can't destroy
If not by the girl, then certainly by the boy
I've found stupid stacked on smart
Till you couldn't see either or tell them apart

Just like circles that never end
Cycles over and over again
Never happy with what we choose
Never learn by what we lose

The Introduction

She moved with great ease to and fro
as she pleased
To every mans delight
The grace was there, the coast was clear,
I felt the time was right.

I adjusted my posture as I stood there
and watched her.
As her smile flashed to a grin
I don't want to be forward,
although, I think I ought to,
but who wants to just go barging in.

I looked at my shoes and my finest
dress blues
And I knew my shape was trim
I waited my turn as I knew I would
earn
That moment when I'd go marching
in.

Standing right there, her skin so fair,
I couldn't help but fix my gaze.
Emotions rise and fall with the thought
of it all
A trail opened through the crowd like a maze

I shifted my weight as I thought
what fate.
Me, this moment and all
I thought, what should I do as I looked down
at my shoe
Then back to the clock on the wall.

Maybe I'd better speak up?
I looked her way, all callers at bay,
I adjusted my tie, I sipped from my
Cup

Suddenly more difficult than I had dreamed,
plotted and schemed
To make this acquaintance some way
I balked and I wavered, I thought and I savored
I fretted and sweated away

When time had passed and then alas
she walked away with him
I felt relief from a pretty thief
Who had stolen my night since ten.

My Illusion

She said she would be here by ten
I watched the crossing sign change then change again
People coming and going there own special ways
I seemed to be the only stillness found in the maze

Cold and windswept I kept my place
Searching the crowd for that familiar face
So many faces coming at me
Yet never the face I wanted to see

Lengthy moments come and gone
I stood with faith, I stood forlorn
The crowd subsided as my anticipation diminished with time
I became painfully aware, that our meeting
Was just an illusion of mine

Dance with the Devil

All else pales when a lover feels
A third has come into sight
And for each one that cares
another will dare
Come and dance with me tonight

Come dance for the moment
Come dance for the rhyme
Come dance with another
And share a good time.

Just this once come dance a dare
Like there was no other
Come, be mine this time
Let's forget about your lover

Come dance in your golden fabric
Beneath the moons pale light
Dance to the music of temptation
Come dance with me tonight

Come follow the steps of others
These tempestuous steps of mine
Come share with me your loveliness
Come share with me your time

Let's forget the strings that lovers bring
They always seem to bind
Come be free and dance with me
And mix your joys with mine.

Tomorrow is your wish
My desire is only for tonight
Come dance away your treasures
To the moons generous light

See how light on your feet
When you forget a lovers plight
Whirling and spinning the dreams
you dream
As you dance a dare tonight

I will always beckon the beauties
And bargain the jewels that be
So come dance for the devil tonight
Come dance this dance with me.

Leader's Club

There were the years of school and some of the kindest people I would ever know. Mrs. Newmark, Mr. Gould, Mrs. Koerner, Mrs. Schwartz who tried to give me a beautiful coat that my pride could not accept. Nor could I assess the school's opinion that she could not tutor me alone but must include others which destroyed a goodness and spirit she was not allowed to share with me. I still think of her.

Yet time has not allowed me to forget the bad ones. The ones who smacked my face, the gym teacher who spoke gently to this new arrival, and chose to humiliate me in front of all. Smallest boy in class who came from the wrong school. "You wops from the North side wear olive oil in your hair", the Italian gym teacher shouted, as he dragged me by the hair down the stairs to the alcove and threatened me. Tears in my eyes and tears in my heart. I never forgot the teacher, like an ugly scar that has to be worn on ones face. Like the broken nose he chose to have his personal favorite bestow on such a small boy. When he chose them up for a boxing match he created a restless hate, one that would not go away, not ever.

It was the year 1961, as he spoke of the magnificent German breed while he spilled lies on 13 year old children and their impressionable souls.

When the gym master learned that I was on the honor roll, he "invited" me to join the Leaders Club of gymnasts. It wasn't until many years later that I learned the "Leaders Club" in German meant "Fuehrer's Club" and once again it hurt me.

To be a member of this club you had to buy a sweat shirt and "T" shirt emblazoned with "Leaders Club". There was so little money, but some had to be spent there.

A broken nose, broken shoes, broken heart for those who lose.

Walk to School

Red bricks, red bricks and cobble stone
City streets and me all alone

Slate on the walkway, poor gray stone
Worn over time and me all alone

Off to school my first day too!
Feeling all the fears as small boys do

Sidewalks lead to old front door
All new faces and rules to explore

Found the kids who were not kind
Turned away and paid no mind

Angry gym teacher seemed to dare
Pushed me away and pulled my hair

A solemn walk on the way back home
Worn slate sidewalks and me all alone

Natures Domain

In my yard life is hard
As beautiful as my yard can be
Green and soft with birds aloft
Dotted and potted with flowers and trees

Where the sun glows while the crows crow
And the birds sing anonymously
The trees whisper like older sisters
They hover over me

Here the cats chase mice and shorten their life
And my dog will not let the cats be,
A wild turkey's clutch with a fox that does what he must,
I saw the fight there in front of me

There where the butterflies thrive
Amongst the honey suckle and rye,
I saw the oriole swallow a butterfly
And steal that joy from me

And the robin built his nest
There under my deck
But my son just wouldn't let it be

So I watch and yawn
As these things go on
Amongst the beauty I see

It makes some things perfectly clear
Like the soft summer air
Or the sting of the honey bee

The Old Dog

Seems like the old dog is getting mean,
Hate to see him change that way
I saw him nip at little Johnnie
For almost no reason today

You know they grew up together
The old dog shouldn't act that way
I remember when Johnnie would ride his back
And pull his ears to make the hound bay

They would play for hours
And the old dog never got mean
Now I've lost faith
Because of what I've seen

I remember the times,
Johnnie could do anything to that dog
Take away his food
Or roll him like a log

Never growled, never nipped
Never once got mean
Surely one of the greatest dogs
I have ever seen

But now everybody is concerned
All have lost their trust
Nobody seems to feel comfortable
The old dog has gone bust

We sure did like him
Except when he grew mean
Something inside made him snap
Judging by what I've seen

Afraid of such behavior
The old dog just isn't any more
Now we have a cute new pup
And once again, something to adore

The Moments We Look Back

Some memories are kind and some are dear,
some are fleeting and some quite clear,
There are those best left unattended in the grayness of time,
Less pain, less hurt, no pictures to remind.

Although there amongst the shadows lies a marker of mine,
Relentless and unforgiving the hurt I left behind.
Who would ever believe that I would grieve stepping over the line,
That I would smart, so many years apart, for that endless stinging time.

So be aware of some things the future may bring,
It's memories may not be kind.
What we now create is for futures sake
In the moments we look behind.

Factory Rat

We pulled up and parked a short distance from the front door. John was at the wheel. We parked in a shady spot under some large trees. On one side of the street was a red brick grammar school set in the sun. Next to it was a row of factories set in the shade. Across the street was Watsessing Park with its cool green blanket covering everything in sight. A brook ran alongside just beyond the iron picket fence. The brook was Wigwam Brook a fact little known by most. It was the very same brook that meandered through several small towns. It was the same brook that ran behind my house on East Day Street when I was a boy. Slow moving, gurgling brook that ran all the way to the river I played in as a boy. It ultimately emptied in the bay Down Neck.

This brook was a gentle peaceful part of my life, but when the clouds rolled in and the rains came the soothing nature of this brook revolted. It revealed distaste for being crowded and contained to its low lying bed. The brook climbed out of its shallow bed like a monster flooding all but the high ground, reclaiming what was once its domain and took lives like an angered god. I once saw it leap from its banks lash out, and take Peter away.

"Are you really going in that door and make yourself a factory rat for the rest of your life?" John asked with a form of disbelief in his voice. The reply was soft and punctuated with uneasiness, "Yeah, I'm going in, I'm going to start here, right here!", as I closed the car door behind me. Looking back through the open window, I said, "don't wait, I'll walk home."

The machines hummed like a hive. Busy bees filling, capping, labeling bottles and tubes, flowing round and round on a carousel until they had their fill. Sent off, marching in lines toward the waiting women, sitting about in camp fire style, picking and packing, chattering as they filled the boxes with the liquid gold that fed them all. They pushed the finished product toward this small frail young boy, moving and swaying to the rhythm of the day. Small box into big box, day after day, sweating and moving like a manufacturing ballerina. Only the young men were on this side of the line. The older guys were mechanics or gone. Not many cared to dance at the end of the line, nor smell the acrid fume of hair dye. It was a stopping place, although some were captured for life. Like the shop stewart, Jimmy, captured by his alcoholism, his borrowing of small amounts of money and his forgetting to repay. Captured by his wife who worked on line thirty-two and watched him like cat watches a mouse, but he always managed to have a drink as the day progressed.

Hector ran the cream machine, tall lanky Puerto Rican kid, curly black hair sharp features. He had a "who cares" smile on his face when he told me he was leaving. The military called him, "the draft". The much feared draft that stalked like a wolf searching for every young man that wasn't in college and took him away. I soon filled Hectors spot, now I was a mechanic and sent product down the line instead of receiving it. In my own way I enjoyed the challenge of the gears, levers and motion that sent the shimmering dyes, the oxbloods, and blacks clinking along, a virtual orchestra of glass on glass, glass on steel, chatter on chatter. I knew this would only last so long. There was a war raging outside that just took Hector. The American cities were burning from within. The President was afraid of the "domino affect" in Asia while his country burned under his feet.

I was eighteen when I saw the cities burning. It seemed like the war I always felt inside came raging to the surface tearing at everything around me. I felt myself on a tight rope, walking a narrow path that I knew would ultimately lead to the draft, a war, and the burning cities that already surrounded me. Like an industrial ballerina I danced and sweated to the tune of bottles clinking, machines humming, bright colored dyes and the awful breath taking smells of nail polish and industrial chemicals. The job had its' benefits though, like the summertime help. Each year, for ninety days, the college girls arrived and filled the place with something for me to enjoy. I liked this one and that one and they liked me although there was no overlooking the facts. Any relationship was doomed,I was a full timer something that may have befallen their parents but not them. They would be on to something new and presumably wonderful in September. I regretted my plight, yet, understood why I was there. I was not alone but that was not much comfort for me, neither were the other nine months filled with middle aged and old women who generally filled my day with complaining about each other, the mechanics. Flirting with the young boys seemed to help them along, so, I seldom took offense or overlooked the opportunity to make them smile, although there were times I could not muster the patience required to make them or someone like "Big Lil" comfortable.

When I saw the manila envelope and government address, I knew, without opening my mail, the time had come. My world would change. Like the college girls September would bring something new although, for me, it would be dangerous, like walking in a mine field. I tucked the letter in my pocket without opening it and started up the long hallway to the second floor where I lived.
I had to tell my mother, I knew coming home late at night would no longer be an issue between us, but as fate would have it, I remained at the factory.

I listened to my friends who had returned. They showed me pictures of what a .50 caliber could do to those on the other end of the barrel. I saw pictures of black pajamas looking up at the chopper as it hopped over the trees and came down over a field and surprised them. The picture was clear enough to see their eyes and teeth. There were four of them. My friend Lewis said, "We got them all!" I knew almost as many lives were being taken by drugs, jails, and the violence right here stateside. My friends often agreed but they found hell first hand in Asia. Some did not even recognize that which was taken from them, something that replaced their youth with the nightmare of kill or be killed.

Going to School

I looked into the back of the forty foot box. The truck well ran down hill, so when I looked in it all I saw was black against the bright sunshine. I stepped inside and felt the uphill trip and the extreme heat of the morning, in a closed trailer. I walked up to the top of the incline, just behind the tractor empty handed and wondered how I would fill such a huge hole with forty pound boxes. As I walked down hill back to the loading dock, I started sweating. A huge blonde haired fella came into view. I knew this must be the driver. He approached me surveying my lanky one hundred and fifty pound frame, head to toe. "So they sent you to help me", he said with a strong southern drawl." "Yeah, I guess that's what they expect", I said, looking at my new partner and the stacks of boxes waiting on the dock. The boxes had to be hand carried and I felt they could have used a dozen good men, as we loaded box after box. I was soaked with a sweat and the truck was only half loaded. As I exited the truck my lungs were searching for fresh air. The big guy looking down with a superior smile said, "Hey, what's wrong?" "What's wrong?" I replied, "I'm a mechanic, this is not my kind of work." With that big southern smile and drawl he laughed, "hell, I can do this all day," he said. "What time have you got?" I asked "Just about noon", he shot back. "Well that's lunch time for me." "How long is lunch?" he asked. "Half hour," I replied. Throwing his shoulders back with that big broad smile, "take some extra time", he said. "Looks like you need it". I nodded and pulled my sweat soaked shirt free of my chest, hoping some breeze would find its way between me and the soaked cloth.

I took my brown bag and staggered into the park, found that familiar spot under the shade tree and drank the cool breeze like it was water. Now I could feel a chill as I listened to the sound of the large punch presses slaving away. My half hour turned into an hour before I started back. I hoped that truck was loaded and as I climbed the stairs to the dock, I heard a booming voice, "where the hell you been?" The sweating hulk screamed. I smiled and replied, "Lunch".

"Hell, you been gone an hour" glancing at his watch. "Hell, I thought you could do this stuff all day, now you're complaining," I smiled and brushed past him. "Come on let's finish up."

I had saved some money and didn't know where I would get the rest, but I called a school, made an appointment that very day. I went full time for two years at night while working during the day. That truck was a major contributor to my future success. The girl I met and married, my drive to succeed, that factory job, all contributors to a new outlook on life.

Always a Balance

There were times I couldn't help giving life a tweak
Changing times and changing lives, by merely changing seats

Climbing in the ring to face the bruising bout
Knowing that putting in was balanced with taking out

Going up was always part of coming down
Peace in the world was the absence of sound

Truth was evasive but something that could be
But always different for you, always different for me

A Factory Lunch

Here's a place for me
At the base of this old tree
The roots like fingers stretched from a palm

Beckon come rest your body, share my calm
Wrinkled brown bag with a simple lunch

And a shady spot where the leaves did bunch
Sometimes I'm hungry even when I'm done
Times I was hungry, when there was none

And when I consider the shape of things
I'm glad I know what a tree can bring.

And as the ant discovers a crumb
I know, out in the field, an ant has none.

And there behind me, the factories buzz
Deep inside with bright red blood
Some young and some old
With hands of grease, and hands of gold

And as the breeze flutters my clothes
I stare out in the field, where the flowers grow
And my thoughts turn to her

Way down deep where the emotions stir.
In that private spot where no one goes
Where I keep my pride and poets clothes

I know she has never thought of me.

Down deep where her spot would be.

And when the time came she did go.

Kind of, out in the field where the flowers grow

The world would spin,

And the sun would shine

And the loss I knew was only mine.

And back inside the monster roars

It wants more blood from this young boy.

Love is for Those Who Dare

Love is so delicate
Like the dancing flame that clings to the candle's wick
So prone to lose its footing
So close to being interrupted
By all things that surround it

Clinging to the wick for life
Changing shape and color in the darkness
Fragile flower lighting the way
For those who dare or take a chance

For those who recognize loves vulnerability
Balanced by its joy
And so often, time permitting
It's eventual tear filled demise

Sometimes extinguished by the whim
The unexpected invisible breeze
Carrying sad surprise
For those who dare to love

No Man's Land

I sit and stare aimless; eyes fixed on the dirt wall
So close to my face, so covered in blood that it's grains stick to me as
though we were one.

Frozen amongst the madness, moved only by the exploding shells that
make the ground shutter endlessly,
like a passing train.

Consciously pushing aside the death and despair lying at my feet,
buried deep in my memory, my sole, my tears,
While my world clouds thick with the ever-present smell of powder
and rotting flesh.
I am consumed by the dark line of trenches;
one on one, one on more, trench on trench, war on war.

Dug deep into the earth and mixed with mother's blood, young boys
and soldier's toys the endless sea of mud, the fears and final moments
for the frightened and the brave.

Crowned by a sea of barbed wire I shiver in soldiers' grave.
There in blackened field glowing above my head reds and yellows, the
frightening whites,
the seeking, the hiding, the living and the dead.

Staring at the wall, night above my head, sticky blood running in my
eyes, my life,
the living and the dead.
I no longer have the strength to look, the torture too much to bear, the
silhouettes hung on barbed wire only thunder my despair.

The lifeless jagged geometries like so many darkened puzzle pieces are
hung
on the landscape,
Like twisted scarecrows to remind all those that dare to live.
It's here I sit and stare at the wall, shaking, mixing blood and dirt on
my hands.

Mud about my feet, my uniform, and each dead man.

The Cost of Freedom

I knew my country proud and tall
And as a boy I answered the call
We carried the torch for freedoms fare
Here at home and everywhere

We gave our sons, we gave our dreams
Here at home and in-between
First a revolution, then a Civil War
Then came bleeding on foreign shore

On their soil we spilled our blood
We left our souls, we spent our sons
The losses always much greater than gain
Except for the freedoms we now retain

And when I see our flag
I know what it means
Buried deep beneath those colors
Is the cost of freedom's dream

Flags are for the Eye

On the highest hill in the cemetery
a brilliant flag flies
And right below waves another
two thousand
For those who had to die

And the rows of bright colors flying
Bring no comfort for those who
eternally lie.
Because the ground is for the dead
The flags are for the eye.

And somehow I can't help feeling
guilty
With death before me spread from
eye to eye
And the flags humming like bees
As memories come rushing by

I know they were just average men
Caught in a place and time
Imagine the first wave
Or the bomber brigade
Or standing on a mine

So I know these flags mean
more than courage
They mean more than decoration
can buy

They mean more than most care to

give

Yet they did it and they died

So I won't speak of causes

Or the nobility of pride

For I know I stand on the blood

of ages

Right here where these soldiers lie

I hope no more is taken

My sons or daughters, you nor I

It just seems so strange for those who

remain

These flags are for the eye

About To Die

I lay here on my back

Eyes open

Staring at the sky

The final position
For a man about to die

A time to wonder
Where will I go
Where have I been
Who am I

Alone without a friend
Am I at the starting gate?
Or the ominous finish line?

Never found my place
In this maze
In this rhyme
Lying here
Staring at the sky
Taking nothing with me
No place to hide

How very singular
This very last ride
Waiting staring at the sky

The Diner

He worked his factory shift three thirty to eleven pm

Then he headed for the time clock, he headed for the open air

He knew he would be back again, tomorrow

So he headed for the freedom one feels when their thoughts and attentions flow into the streets

The world of late night diners, cheap women, the smell of perfume, of fresh brewed coffee, fried onions and burgers which fill one's nostrils and stomach refreshing the memories of last night's luck

The lady fair he met right there, who had run amuck

They shared their lives and so many lies in the back seat of his car, back seat of her life for a moment, maybe once, maybe twice

But tonight the diner furnished no trophies as he stared into a lonely cup of java and his reflection in the diner's window the neon light flashing on and off

hid nothing from the truth, it told no lies

Just a reflection of so many frowns and sighs found on the faces of so many late night guys

John Spangler's Fate

Quiet green hills and granite
Memories for the eye
Set above the awesome woe
Set below a satin sky

Here lies John Spangler
He made this grass mound a home
And for all he found in life
When John Spangler died
John Spangler died alone

Here lie the dreams of tomorrow
The fears of yet to come
The trees were filled with whispers
Tomorrow and yet tomorrow is done!

Soldier Boys

There amongst the markers placed
I wade waist high
Above the reminders of death
Marked by banners steeped in pride

Even though there were no voices
Someone began to cry
There amongst the small white crosses
The soldier boys and I

Rows and crosses
Crosses and rows
The mothers sons
That each man knows

And at each memorial
A tiny flag flies
Above the head of each man dead
These soldier boys and I

War

Melted crosses and
forgotten shrines

The scorched earth and
and endless lines

And the relentless madness
the winner waged

Now writes history
and lead the parade

If you have killed many
or if you have killed one

If you have done it for honor
or done it for fun

Or if you have done it
through madness

Like so many deeds are
done

Join the parade
The madness and you are one

The Victor

The winnerless games
And the participants it claims
Lay scattered on the hill
While the victor struts proud
In tattered crowd
Amongst bloodied dream
And lifeless wills

Circus Full of Madness

Circus full of madness, round and round
People creating sadness,
Sadness creating sound,

Artists painting feelings
The crying out loud
Posing as the actor, posing as a clown

Circus full of madness round and round

The Fighter's Madness

As I sit this darkened day, blood
Stained and more
I feel the war once again coming
To the surface

Bursting, raging, confused, like
The beaten fighter
Scraping air, scraping air, in his
Blind madness

Clawing, holding on to the violence
Before him
He must not lose, he must not
Lose

And every blow he takes brings
Him closer to freedom

Because madness truly cannot
Recognize a loser

And here I sit still with the sense
To ponder
Veteran of many an ordeal

Still not able to wrench right from
Wrong
Good from bad, this from that

And time always the enemy
And embrace, creeping, moving
Into all corners
Changing everything it touches

Like the dancing flame of the
Roaring fire
Taking lives, taking lives
Endless drain.

A Nice Apartment

It was a nice apartment, one room, wood floors, bathroom, small kitchen, two windows, a small alcove in which to set up my easel and a less than modest turntable for the few records I had. This three story garden apartment became a peaceful island nestled on the border of the lush green park.

Below the window, between the buildings was a garden with a bench on which some solitary soul would occasionally perch and play a flute. It sounded like a bird below, in the canyon beyond my window, beyond the fire escape far from the sounds of the city. This small world was a place to rest, to file some of the memories that I need not visit anymore, the unpleasant ghosts that they were.

Deep inside where no one was allowed to go, I was still lonely but happy to have found some of the small freedoms I was able to know. I would take a quiet walk in the park, which oddly enough had a continuation of the same waterway that flowed through my childhood, past the factory, to the river where I dreamed and played as a boy.

Now a young man, once again at rivers edge, taking a moment in time, in the cool depths of the shade tree. Standing there, I could see my reflection, my memories and regrets. I was no longer a boy. For once in my life I did not see the reflection of my brother nearby nor feel the pain that John carried with him and spread like wet paint. John was dead and the only pain now, was the memory that he left behind.

The Dope

The dope has taken him away
And I can no longer reach him

There are too many horrors between us
I am a lone survivor
at the end of a bitter journey
through someone else's hell

He was destroyed, easily taken down
by the strongest poison we would ever know

When the smallest slip of slips
would not let him go.

He was devoured, taken away, silenced,
Forever.

A Couple Bags of Stuff

It's a dirty little alley
But that is just what he needs
To shrink from inquisitive eye
Perform his lustful deed

Not doing well
Things are really rough
Sitting in an alley
On a couple bags of stuff

It's a confused place
Things are scattered without order
But inside that garbage can lid
He knows he'll find some water

There on a can
He cleared a little spot
Laid down his joints, cooker and stuff
Then tied up for a shot

A fly kept buzzing about
Making circles above his head
If he'd land even for a moment
The bastard would be slapped dead

He took a few swats in the air
The fly wouldn't go away
So he dumped the dope in the cooker
And let the rascal play

He lit on his ear
Then walked down his cheek
Back to his ear
As though to speak

He checked out the lid
But the water wasn't clear
So as long as it cooked with the dope
He didn't really care

He sucked up the water with the dropper
Scurried back to his seat
Splashed it into the cooker
And gave it some heat

The matches nipped at his fingers
The burn well worth the high
Then back on his lower lip
Landed that bastard fly

He blew at the fly
While concentrating on the shot
Nothing could distract him now
Or take away his lot

When the last speck dissolved
He put the cooker down
Blew more air at the fly
which knocked him to the ground

He pushed the joints onto the dropper,
drew up the liquid gold
The fly was now forgotten,
The annoyance had grown old

His tattered veins swelled up at him
Just begging to be filled with stuff
But he deliberately picked up his cigarette
He took a slow easy puff

Time was no longer important
The world was at his feet
He had all there was to be had
Or all there was to be

He waited just long enough
Now time to get down
To tip of the set he placed his finger
Then shook it to the ground

Pushing it in that familiar spot
The steel found the tattered vein
He was jolted by that familiar surge
Something he couldn't tame

He threw back his head
Closing his swollen eyes
He sat in slackened pose
Unaware of his demise

His head no longer up
Everything moving down
He was no longer getting high
But falling to the ground

This had happened before
A penalty of his needs
But things kept growing stronger
No longer could he breathe

Suddenly all movement subsided
The dope had ceased to yield
Ruthless thief in a dirt alley
With mothers son to steal

The fly had gone away
No longer was it near
Like all the distractions found in life
things finally ended here

To most a savage beast had fallen
But to me it was someone I knew well
Someone who ran away from an empty life
and died in a garbage strewn hell.

Sitting in Autumn

The leaves blew like snowflakes
In the cool autumn air

Forming a golden crown upon
All that was green
In the spirit of autumn cheer

And as I sit and watch the show
And the performers that are near

I lose myself in the autumn leaves
This special time of year

That Subtle Slippage

When Fall arrives the morning sun is filtered by Autumn mist
The days grow short, more darkness than light
Golden arrays stretch across the landscape, short lived
and dinned by the on coming

There is a cold subtle slippage into winters' darkness
Like a love that has gone bad, almost unnoticed, winter is here.

The Feelings of Autumn

Autumn nips the summer air
and fills it with a chill
It fills skies with birds
on high
And the seasons changing will

It always colors the green with
reds and yellows and shades
between

With pumpkin and corn the
fields adorn
a time of Halloween

A time when shadows appear from the other
side
They color my sweater
They color my stride

A sky of blue behind it all
A rustling of leaves
and the migration call

Autumn feeds the memory
With colors and feelings
And the things you see

Michael's Glass Eye

It was a warm February night and the steam rose up off the snow to form a fog that was almost comforting, like when snow falls. I sat still and quietly spoke almost in a hum and my friend seemed to hum back discussing our lives. It was a quiet time looking beyond the fog, looking at our place in life, a truthful time.

"Do you ever want to get married, Vic", Michael asked. I was hesitant to reply as he peered through the fog as though looking for answers. "I don't see it doing anything for me". "I have nothing to give, Michael, and who have you ever liked that just takes?" "I know a lot of those guys", Michael said as he grew uncomfortable with my bringing up the subject. "Something like that is big, Mike." "It means a lot of things and I don't think I have ever loved anything, it just doesn't happen". "It seems to fool and hurt more people than it helps, I feel, but that's all".

Michael was a young man, a glass eye. His father drunk, full of rage and hatred hit Mike so hard he lost his eye when he was just nine years old. I knew Michael, like me, had scars that would not go away. But unlike Mikes' father, my father did not leave me blind, just alone. There was a pause, then Mike started again, "Yeah but you're a smart dude Vic, people know that, people like you, chicks too. You've got more on the ball than most of the cats I know. Shouldn't be so hard on yourself man." I knew if Mike thought there was no future for his friend it would dampen any hopes he might have for himself.

I changed the subject, "beautiful night though". "Yeah" Michael said looking back and forth. It seemed like Michael wanted something more from me, something better than what he had heard so far. "What about that chick that comes down to see you all the time?" "What about her?" I replied kind of annoyed. "Well, I mean she likes you, you know." "Yeah I know," I replied.

"Here's half a buck go get a container of beer." Beer for off premise consumption was only sold in white card board containers, on Sunday, in those days. Free beer was something Michael was always interested in, even more than my love life. He scooped up the change from my hand and disappeared in the mist.

I was left to my thoughts. I knew fifty cents would buy me a brief pause from the questioning, at least until Michael returned with the beer.

I Wanted

I wanted a soda but the machine was broken
I wanted a ride but had no token

I wanted to hear but no word was spoken
I wanted to go up but kept coming down

I wanted to go straight but kept going round
I wanted to believe better could be found

I wanted some sincerity but always a clown
I wanted some truth to keep around

I wanted something better yet never found
I wanted a love I could feel was true

I wanted to color these endless blues
That's when I found it just standing there

With torn blue jeans and light brown hair
With a smile for me as I stood in the rain
She recognized the need and erased the pain

A Lovers' Patience

For all the pain I've found in life
I found love too!

I found it along the way,
I found it knowing you.

But I found you crying last night,
as lovers sometimes do

And the pain that I know
is part of loving too!

Nothing can be so perfect
that it is always right for you,

And even love, the greatest thing,
will sometimes make that true.

In Love

Watching the patterns on my
window pass

The rain drops bring life to a
lifeless glass

Changing and moving without a sound
they bring me comfort when you're
not around

So I find myself perched on
a sill

The rain drops like dreams dancing
at will

Patterns and colors and things
Unclear

Like the loves I have known through out
the years

Yet I feel warm as I watch the rain
happy to be in love again

Great Day

What a great day!
What a great sky
With a gentle breeze
A bird sails by

I hear their muddled calling
Off in the distant sphere
Separate from the people world
Sent to lighten my cares.

And it's great to be in love
The grandest care of all
The color of the sky
The laughter of the gull

The motion of the water
And the sound it rushes in
The changing of the tide
The rustling of the wind

The laughter of those playing
The smiles and the grins
And the open sea before me
All reflect the love I am in.

And here on this timeless beach
To most I appear alone,
But it is here I blend my love,
My perceptions and my poems

High Flying Things

Sometimes when I'm chasing
High flying things

Opening every door
And shaking all that rings

I lose sight of the common things
And the complexity that may bring

I forget all the songs that
Sad people sing

When I'm chasing those high flying
Things

Duke Fishing

The water was smooth and flat, like a large horizontal pane of black glass. It seemed like there was no movement except the oars slowly skipping over the surface of the water, creeping along the shore line. Hunting, listening to Dukes whispered instruction. We were probing for the elusive bass in the black of night. This was all new to me and I had no idea of what to expect. As a boy I had caught small Kellies in a net or even by hand on the banks of the river. I had sometimes found large numbers of eels that came up the river to spawn but as a young boy I didn't fully understand that either, nor why they disappeared.

On this night I found myself sliding along a foreign shoreline casting a lure at what I did not know, but I anxiously waited for a tug on the line. Behind Duke I could see the moon and its' reflection on the lake and the tops of the pine trees pointed like arrows at the moon. I was sliding along in a world so quiet, so foreign, so beautiful, I felt like I was peering through a hole at someone else's world. It was Dukes world and he pulled me through the hole onto another plane, from which I would find a new spirit, a new way.

The calm that surrounded us suddenly exploded into a violent eruption as my tiny lure met the shore line. I thought a large animal darted from the bushes and jumped at us and then suddenly, as quick as it started, it stopped. Whirling my head about in a defensive posture I saw no reaction from Duke which surprised me. Duke calmly and quietly said, "You missed him Vic"! "Missed what?" I replied, confused, even frightened. You missed your first bass. I knew at that moment I had just passed through an open door with no regrets and there was a life as new as being reborn. I also knew a door closed behind me, there on the lake, in the black of night, heart pounding in the light of the moon.

Night Flight

Silhouettes streak silently across the moonlit landscape,

All is quiet and cool, I become part of their passing flight

Comfortable and alone I sit in a calm spot this autumn night

But I am witness to the journey, shrouded in darkness and the moons silvery
light

I long for the moving on, for the stealing away in darkness

Yet my journey is as secret as it is endless

So I sit alone as these reflections of life silently steal by

I have a moment is spent on the wing.

Nature's Song

I love to sit and feel
the breeze
Watch it bend and shape
the trees
As it moves across the lake
it fills the sails
Their colors great

Off in a distance it has
a song
As it rustles the flag
all day long
As the people stand
and cheer
It carries their message
way over here
It shapes the grass
shiny then green
It lifts the bird till
barely seen.

Oh! How I love the breeze so clean
a touch and taste yet
never seen.
And the joy it
Often brings
A song so sweet that
Nature sings

Shadows

Shadows hiding in distant trees
Beneath the boughs, between the leaves

Shadows darting here and there
Between the people and everywhere.

It follows me and the children too!
Through the neighborhood off to school

Sometimes, I like to play
Making shapes in the strangest ways

Me and my shadow, we have no cares
My closest friend throughout the years

Ah the shadow is a happy time
Like the butterfly and the children's rhyme

And for all the darkness shadows bring
They add to the joy of
simple things.

Nighttime

Night is the time when darkness fills all corners
Like a fluid running, seeping, searching out

Filling all voids with greedy intent
Like the spoiled child that must have his way

Giving passage to all those who care to remain unnoticed
Those who stay hidden away with the advantages found in darkness

Nighttime is when strange things come alive, colorless
Live shadows moving about faceless, nameless

Moving in, moving out
Stealthy invader, relentless shroud

Smothering all appearances
With its endless darkened veil

It Was Me

I saw them reaching out
So I gave them my hand
It kept them from falling behind

I saw them falling away
When I grabbed them by the seat of their pants
Despite their breach entry
They came through and subsequently brought others

When I saw them peering through the crack in the fence
I showed them how to climb over
When I saw those not interested in the other side
I made noise to arouse their curiosity
Which none is without

When they became beleaguered or forlorn
I used music, marches and love songs
To move them along

For some reason I felt it necessary to help
the lost or set aside when there is plenty for all.
I felt none should be without or left behind

When the great indecision came,
When I was challenged,
I looked in the mirror and realized
All of them were me.

Up the Mountain

Going up the mountain
It's just blue sky
Opportunity springing like fountains
For this young guy

Don't know east
Don't know west
Don't know going down
Don't know "nothing left"

Just going up to reach my peak
Looking for the top
and the things I seek
No rear view mirror
To take a peek

Moving on, moving up
Full grown dog from helpless pup
Faster and stronger as I can be
Up the mountain to see what I can see

I've heard the stories
I've seen the men
Somewhere long ago
Can't remember when

Just moving up toward blue sky
Me and my friends, apple pie
But one happy day I reached the top

No more looking up; straight ahead
An awesome drop

And I remembered the stories,
the men I had seen
Somewhere long ago
When I was living the dream

Life Goes On

"Good morning Victor", a great big smile flashed across her face. "I need your signature on these documents. The drawing package is almost complete, they're working on them now. I'll need you to review and signature them too. Then I'll send them out." It was Mary my faithful young executive secretary, very attractive, very laden with a pregnancy, very soon to deliver. Her broad smile always gave me a feeling of comfort, as though everything was "ok". "Sure", I shot back, glancing up at her, "let's start the day!" I scribbled my name in the lower right hand corner where she pointed intently. Then I leaned back in my chair, staring at Mary, which went unnoticed by her as she inspected my signature. "Mary when is your last day?", as though I didn't know. I dreaded not being greeted by that big smile each morning, but by this time in life I was well worn to the notion of change. "Two more weeks" she said, without looking up as she turned and exited the office. I sat still for a moment then spun around and stared out the window.

She reminded me of her, the only real love I felt I had ever known. I stared out at the clear blue sky, the hills in the distance and the lush green meadow just below my window. Right through the center ran a river, not the same one I had always known but it meandered through the meadow and through my life each day. It reflected like a mirror in the morning sun today and most days. Once again my thoughts turned to her and a kaleidoscope of memories flashed through my consciousness. My thoughts were interrupted by a reflection jumping off my gold watch but I continued to stare out. Off in a distance a flock of starlings formed a pattern that shifted and changed like a windblown sheet hung on a clothes line. I stared down at my shoes as though I were searching for something lost. The familiar phrase, nothing will ever be the same came to mind. I knew that to be true, except for that familiar feeling that I would have to go it alone.

Nothing ever took away that feeling of loss. I came to accept that which most people find so dreadful. Everything gained is ultimately lost or dissolved along the way sometimes with very little fanfare or notice and life goes on.

Winters Chill

I will never forget
how Winter's chill crept inside my
clothing
And lay its soft white blanket at my feet

The trees appeared as spun crystal
So fragile, and silent against a
darkened sky.

It was then that I met her,
and it was then that I loved her.
Now, once again, the loneliness
of loves gone by; forever

Yesterday

I remember autumn leaves
The wind rushing through her hair
Pictured glances golden yellow
The cool frosty air
The smell of the earth
The blue sky, my feelings within
The gains and the losses
The thick and the thin
Sometimes without a smile,
I think of yesterday

Despair

We shared hopes and tomorrows
We gathered and built upon love
When some things seemed so far away

She was what I had searched for
That very special one
That fell within my humble reach

I long for her and I know she is gone
Back to the emptiness from which
she came
What seemed to be my only joy
And it can never be the same.

Sometimes I look for her
In other times and faces

Forlorn, I know, I will not
find her there

And the scent left on the pillow
Only chooses to heighten my despair
These thoughts of her, and my
solitary longing,
Are something I cannot escape

Now life's joys have become
just fleeting glances

And I, one of life's, endless
swinging gates.

The Wind is A Reminder

The wind keeps rushing my way
Tugging my hat and crowding
the day

My clothes it fills with
endless flutter
The colored leaves chase
one another

Across the field and round again
Tumbled in the air and tumbled
in the glen

The wind brings strange
sounds to a quiet boy
And hastened speed to sailing
toys

To me it brings a somber tone
Whistling through the trees
and all alone

There were times I had no cares
Once a young fella, now many
years

The things I still treasure
of the many I have known
The smiling face and caring eyes
The place she made called home

And I miss her, most of all
When the winter turns to spring
and summer turns to fall

And I'm glad she was never as
lonely as I

She had a loving friend till the day she died

And who ever thought, that I
Would allow the wind, to make me cry

9 781950 948000